WHY CAN'T I PLAY LIKE JIMMY?

GUITAR RUT REMEDIES

MICK COSTELLO

Copyright © 2022 Mick Costello

All rights reserved. No part of this publication may be reproduced, distributed, or transmitted in any form or by any means, including photocopying, recording,
or other electronic or mechanical methods, without the prior written permission of the publisher, except in the case of brief quotations embodied in critical reviews and certain other noncommercial uses permitted by copyright law.

Costello, Mick (author)

WHY CANT I PLAY LIKE JIMMY:
GUITAR RUT REMEDIES

ISBN: 978-1-922803-88-7

Self Development for Musician

Typesetting - Calluna Light 11/14
Book design by Green Hill Publishing

A GUITAR IS SOMETHING THAT YOU CAN HOLD AND LOVE AND IT'S NEVER GOING TO BUG YOU. BUT HERE'S THE SECRET ABOUT THE GUITAR – IT'S DEFIANT. IT WILL NEVER LET YOU CONQUER IT. THE MORE YOU GET INVOLVED WITH IT, THE MORE YOU REALISE HOW LITTLE YOU KNOW.

LES PAUL

CONTENTS

Why Can't I Play Like Jimmy?	5
Myths Busted	13
Breakthrough Barriers	15
Practice Mindset	24
Stranger In The Dark	40
The Deep End	44

WHY CAN'T I PLAY LIKE JIMMY?

About Me

I spent a lot of my youth chasing the intense atmosphere of loud music and sweaty mosh pits, while avoiding school at all costs. I had family connections to one of the most prominent gig promoters in town, and they hooked me and my brother up with free tickets and occasionally jobs with the site crews. One of the first concerts I ever attended was the Big Day Out in 1999.

I'll never forget the line-up that year. I thought I was the luckiest kid alive (my brother and I were the only kids there). While my friends were at school staring at a chalk board trying to stay awake during algebra lessons (whatever that is) I was in amongst rowdy crowds of sweaty and drunken revellers watching Marilyn Manson, Korn, Soulfly, Ramstein, and many others rock out on the big stage.

Some of the reactions I got from people in the crowd that year were priceless. One shirtless guy with his T-shirt wrapped around his head said, "hey, look at this little dude" and then just picked me up and threw me straight on top of the crowd, over the barriers, and into the arms of security who then asked me where my parents were.

That day changed my life and was the start of a yearly ritual until the festival's slow death after 2010.

I knew all I wanted to do from then on was shred on the guitar. The rock stars made it look so easy and effortless.

After begging my parents, I got my first acoustic guitar for my twelfth birthday. I could barely put the thing down and I started to figure out some riffs by listening to songs on the radio and some cassette tapes I had.

I would pretend my bedroom was the Big Day Out main stage and used the imagination only a kid with a big dream knew how to. From there, I would take my guitar everywhere with me and loved when other kids would show me a new riff, chord, or technique.

In high school I formed a short-lived death metal band in my parents shed, terrorising my family and neighbours ear drums and obliterating any serenity the quite street once enjoyed.

One time, we snuck into the high school music room at lunch and started jamming. Before we knew it, the room was packed with kids, watching and head banging. The windows were even covered with faces looking in from the outside. When the music teacher returned after hearing this abomination of everything she tries to teach, the room was cleared in a stampede of kids running out the door with instruments flying all over the place.

It was the closest I have ever been to rock stardom. Shortly after, I left the band and found other interests (some of which I don't recommend). I didn't play much guitar during that time, apart from the occasional jam at a party or around the campfire.

I always played the same old songs, riffs, and chord progressions I learnt all those years ago.

One day when I was watching a cover band play Led Zeppelins Rock and Roll, I got that old feeling again and said to myself

"WHAT THE HELL AM I WAITING FOR?"

The next day, after sleeping off another brutal hangover, I got out my old, banged-up acoustic guitar covered in Big Day Out and surf brand stickers and picked up where I left off all those years ago.

It has since snowballed into a good addiction. Along with working full time and supporting a family, I've managed to find and create precious time to practice and get better consistently.

By swapping time-wasting, unfulfilling activities for guitar practice, I've been able to get better doing what I love without sacrificing my responsibilities.

Along the way, I have developed a practice and motivational guide based on the things that have worked for me over the years, and I hope to share this with you and help unlock your potential.

Enter The Guitar Rut

> *"If you play just one note, you are a musician.*
> *Rome wasn't built in a day.*
> *Guitar ruts are all part of the journey."*

When you feel like giving up, that's the best time to push on. Ruts in your playing and progress will come and go no matter how good you get.

The guitar rut has claimed many players, and deep within its chasm lies talent and creativeness that will remain there for eternity.

Every guitar player encounters ruts in their playing at different stages of their journey. It's simply part of the process. If you don't find a remedy for it, then you'll just avoid your guitar like it's your high school crush.

Many times, I've sat there and said to myself "why can't I play like Jimmy?" After reading some rock star biographies, I know why.

WHY CAN'T I PLAY LIKE JIMMY?

Solid momentum on guitar progress can come to a crashing halt that lasts a lifetime if you don't do something about it before your motivation fades away.

Some of the reasons you might experience a guitar rut are:

- You're challenging yourself too much or not enough.
- You're not learning anything new and playing the same things.
- You're overwhelming yourself trying to learn and practice too much.
- You're sticking to just one style.

Sometimes just learning some chord and scale variations can add some cool new sounds and motivate you to press on. Set aside some time to experiment with the guitar and unlock your unique sound and style.

One of the best things you can do to overcome a rut is to seek others to jam with. Always be inspired by better players, observe them, and pick their brains for tips and knowledge. Never be intimidated by them. You will learn so much by jamming with better players and if you're the better player, then you need to teach, it's your duty. Teaching others will make you a better player and you'll learn more about yourself in the process.

Learning and teaching keeps you motivated and there is a lifetime worth of learning on a guitar.

Don't become another casualty of the dreaded guitar rut. Too many guitarists have been consumed and spat out by it. But not you, not this time.

Dimebag Darrell, one of the best in the business, nails it with this quote:

> *"Whenever I get down on my playing,*
> *I just bend a note, shake it and listen.*
> *What I hear sounds so great it makes me*
> *realize that even a rut doesn't suck."*

Getting out of a guitar rut can be as simple as cranking up the volume and bending a note.

If you're always the best musician in the room, then you're in the wrong room.

WHY CAN'T I PLAY LIKE JIMMY?

The guitar rut is an inevitable part of the journey, so you have to learn to dig your way out quickly and carry on.

Train yourself mentally to enjoy the challenge and smash your way to where you need to be, one small milestone at a time.

It's time to rock on!

MYTHS BUSTED

Myth: You need natural talent to be a musician.

Rubbish! Don't get me wrong, there are people who are naturally talented in a freakish way, but many of the best have spent countless hours trying and failing to get where they are. It's a popular myth I hear often.

People who develop good practice habits will become better than those with natural talent who don't practice

Myth: I don't have enough time to practice.

Really? How much time do you spend on social media? How much TV do you watch?

The questions are endless. Find some that relate to your lifestyle and re-evaluate your priorities.

Is your musical goal more important than watching some bad acting on TV?

Guitarists can be a strange bunch sometimes. Some people might think you're an unsociable hermit when you hide away practicing, but when they hear you play, they go "wow, I wish I could do that"

It's simple: if you want it, you WILL make the time.

WHY CAN'T I PLAY LIKE JIMMY?

Myth: I'm not good enough to perform.

A very popular myth indeed. Many players simply don't believe they are good enough to perform in front of others. Even as they get better at playing, they continue to think this way.

The thought of performing can be terrifying, but the more you avoid it, the more it weighs you down. It's a big step to make, but anything you've been practicing will sound good to someone somewhere.

BREAKTHROUGH BARRIERS

Are there any barriers holding you back from a breakthrough on your progress?

These are just some that I have seen and experienced myself. Once you address these, you should see a rapid improvement in your playing.

It is especially important to read through these, identify any that apply to you, and snuff them out quick.

Getting frustrated about the time it takes to improve and playing nonstop to become the next Hendrix.

Slow down before you burn yourself out and lose interest. You will find yourself in a never-ending cycle of frustration and dissatisfaction no matter how good you get. You must learn to enjoy the journey and not be obsessed with the destination.

Solution

Have a break from the guitar every now and then and come back with fresh ideas, attitude, and mindset.

Be proud of what you can play, and if you get frustrated at your progress play something you know well to remind yourself that you are not a bad player.

Write down some notes in your diary and celebrate small achievements.

Like anything unique, music requires an investment of time. Every moment will be 100% worth it, I promise, so just be patient, it takes time.

Not having anything to practice / play

We have all been there, sitting with a guitar on your lap, trying to think of something to play, and having a complete mental blank. It always seems to be when there's people watching and waiting for you to play something. It can be a little bit embarrassing, especially if they know you've been practicing.

Solution

This is where something called the 'song pyramid' becomes very useful (see page 35). You should have the songs at the bottom of the pyramid memorised and tattooed in your mind, ready to play at any time and place. When you have that memory blank, think of the pyramid.

Another way is to learn chord progressions back to front so you can confidently make up your own tunes on the spot.

Following too many paths / styles at once and from too many different people

This one gets a lot of players, especially now with so much lesson material all over the internet, YouTube, etc. You learn a cool riff, then part of a song or couple of chords, and then move on.

Before you know it, you have a bunch of unfinished songs that you only know how to play the easy bits of.

I get it. We all want to play like Eddie Van Halen, but trying to take on too much at once will only hold you back and cause frustration and confusion, which will lead to you losing interest. Your guitar will shed a tear while it gathers dust in the closet.

Solution

If you want to become a great guitarist, then pay the fee and learn from a pro. Find a good guitar teacher locally or online, I promise there are lots of good ones out there.

Alternatively, create some playlists on YouTube of the songs and techniques you want to get better at. It can be a bit time-consuming, but it's completely free.

Not challenging yourself

Always set aside some time to play some difficult songs or techniques. If you're consistent, it should only take a few minutes daily to make good progress. These are some of the frustrating moments, but you will thank yourself for having a go and setting the wheels in motion.

Again, think of the song pyramid system.

Solution

Find a song you love that is difficult to play and have a go at learning it. If you have a light at the end of the tunnel, the challenge will be rewarding and fun.

Not setting small, achievable goals

Setting small, attainable short-term goals will keep you constantly focused on the end game.

When you smash these goals, reward yourself and then write down your next set of goals.

It can be a challenge keeping yourself interested and keen all the time, so always make sure you update your goals as you knock them over.

Solution

Write down your goals in a notebook or get a copy of the 90-day musicians diary.

Writing down your progress and achievements will always keep the flame alive and you're more likely to hold yourself to account.

Being too arrogant or stubborn

This is an interesting one and often these players have loads of potential because of the amount of confidence they have. But a lot of the time they bluff their way through situations instead of taking the opportunity to learn.

It is time to eat some humble pie and reach out. This applies to all areas of life: if you constantly believe you know everything, then you will not learn. You may be embarrassed to ask for help, but honestly, nobody else cares.

If you just let it go, then you will be in a constant state of learning. Remember, the person who believes they know everything, learns nothing.

Solution

NEVER STOP LEARNING.
Get that Les Paul quote tattooed on your brain.

Obsessing over better players

Watching some 10-year-old kid shred like a possessed demon on YouTube can make you want to burn your guitar.

Maybe that kid is growing up in a house full of guitars with guitar-playing parents and siblings.

Maybe they get locked in their room and told they cannot leave until they play like Slash. Who knows? Who cares?

Use these moments for inspiration instead: if they can do it, so can you!

Solution

Join a private group on Facebook. There are some good ones full of players of all skill levels offering advice and encouragement to one another.

Focus on your journey, not someone else's.

Preserving your expensive equipment

Seriously! Yeah, that's right, some people avoid playing because they are worried about scratching or damaging their guitar. If this sounds like you then that might be why you're having trouble getting better.

Solution

You should always look after your guitars, but you shouldn't be so worried about the finish getting scratched that you hardly get it out of its hardcase.

Sell it, buy a cheaper one, and use the rest of the money for lessons.

If you're guilty of any of these barriers, then it is time to snap out of it. They could be some of the things that are holding you back from making good, consistent progress.

PRACTICE MINDSET

I've always wondered why so many guitarists give up. Most music teachers say to practice for x-number of minutes a day, but it usually just feels like chore because there's no set routine. If you're serious about getting good at something, you need to adopt a growth mindset. You should get excited whenever you have an opportunity to grow and improve.

When watching interviews with rock stars like Slash and Mark Knopfler, I've noticed that one common thing they all say is "you have to want to do it"

Set short-term goals that pave the journey to your long-term success.

If you think you don't have time, you will find ways to make the time. Part of following your dream is sacrifice. Today, we think we never have time to do the things we love, but if you look a little deeper into your daily habits, you might be surprised.

I know how easy it is to get sucked into dramatic reality-TV or a never-ending series on Netflix. This is the exact kind of thing that can be abolished or reduced to create time.

When I first started to get back into playing the guitar, I found it hard to find time to practice uninterrupted.

I did a total Facebook overhaul and joined some private groups for guitar players. I reduced the time I spent pointlessly scrolling through social media and now nearly every post on my feed is guitar related.

I reduced watching TV dramatically, although I still love watching *Sponge Bob Square Pants* with my kids. The reality shows and terrible acting were out.

Making a few small changes made a big difference and I had more spare time than I could have ever imagined.

Learn to love the journey

This is my all-time favourite quote from the legendary Jimi Hendrix:

> *"Sometimes you want to give up the guitar, you'll hate the guitar. But if you stick with it, you're gonna be rewarded"*

Whenever I get stuck in a rut, I think of this quote and it inspires me to keep going. It's become a brain-tattoo, etched into my mind forever.

I often imagine Jimi sitting alone somewhere, practicing the intro for Voodoo Child and getting frustrated with himself. Then, I'll listen to his live performance at Woodstock and be completely blown away.

Another inspiring moment I often think back on is an interview with Metallica's James Hetfield at guitar centre. He talks about how he used to practice riffs in his car during his lunch break at work. It's that kind of dedication that produces greatness, and I highly recommend it listening to it yourself.

Jimmy Page often had his guitar confiscated by the school principal who also suggested he will amount to nothing by leaving school to pursue a career in music.

A quote from Slash that I love is:

> *"Just plug the f#%! in"*

It really could not be any simpler. When you're playing, anything can happen so just plug in and you might surprise yourself.

There are some great autobiographies and interviews and videos on YouTube where some of the stars have been generous with their time. I suggest checking some out; your favourite guitarists are bound to be on there with some interesting things to say. Reading or listening about your favourite guitarists' early habits can be incredibly inspiring.

All the best players were you at some stage in their journeys, and through practice and motivation have become immortalised as rock gods. Having an idea of how they got to where they are is sometimes very reassuring when experiencing challenges in your progress.

If you practice with a purpose and have a clear path with achievable goals along the way the whole journey will be a lot more fun and rewarding.

The ways in which you can grow your practice mindset are almost endless. There's no one size fits all approach, because everyone has different lifestyles and responsibilities. While trying to come up with some that suit your lifestyle, have a look at some that I found helped maximise my practice time.

- Store your guitars in plain sight around the house. HINT: I have one of mine on a stand under the TV, reminding me of the commitments I made to reducing watching TV.

- Set your screensaver on your phone and computer to pictures of your favourite battle axes. Trust me, it works. The more you're exposed to guitars, the more you think about playing.

Music for me is a very visual art, the more I see anything guitar related the more I anticipate what I might play or learn next. My guitars and amp are set up next to my bed, so I always start and finish my day playing guitar.

If your guitar is there ready to go all the time, you are more likely to practice when you have small amounts of time available; I have all girls in my family, so I get in some practice while I'm waiting for them to get ready whenever we go out.

Set up your practice/jam space. Make it easily accessible, Minimise the set up required, and always make improvements to increase good vibes and efficiency.

- Whatever the situation is, jump at the opportunity to get a little bit of extra practice in. Even five minutes of chord changes or picking technique here and there can make a huge difference. The days of sitting around twiddling your fingers waiting will be long gone once you develop the practice mindset.
- Put up an inspirational poster or two next to your bed or practice area and remember the world needs you to do this. We need more people to tap into their creativeness and share their talent.

- You can practice finger picking and chord changes while talking on the phone or watching TV. Practice scales up and down while reading the newspaper, practice while you're reading this! You will be amazed at how much extra practice you can get in without disrupting your routine.

The Confusion Rut

One of the reasons I've found myself in a guitar rut is confusion. All the strings, notes, chords, scales, and patterns can be overwhelming and seem impossible at times. It seems endless, and you might wonder: "how the hell does Jimmy do it?"

Then someone says you have to try an alternate tuning to get a different style of sound. You could then think: "WHAT! I'M DONE" but just relax. When I'm going through one of my confusion related ruts, I think of the quote from Les Paul:

"A guitar is something that you can hold and love and it's never going to bug you. But here's the secret about the guitar – it's defiant. It will never let you conquer it. The more you get involved with it, the more you realise how little you know."

READ THAT QUOTE UNTIL IT'S TATTOED IN YOUR BRAIN!

Take five minutes at a time before every practice session to learn the notes on the fretboard and you should have it down pat in about 30 days. There are many ways to learn the fretboard. Here are some that I have used and seen others have success with.

- Learn the notes one string at a time up and down the neck.
- The BEADGCF method. Play the notes in that order one string at a time.
- Memorise the notes on the dots.
- Practice all the different octave shapes up and down the neck, one note at a time.

A big thing to learn is the CAGED system. I see confused beginners looking at chord charts they found on the internet with 50 different chords spread over it. Throw it in the bin where it belongs because you don't need it; you will know all those chords if you learn the CAGED system step-by-step.

You might find that some of the chord shapes are difficult and you may never play them, but understanding the system and the patterns are the important thing here. Visualising the patterns on the fretboard will set you free on the guitar and make it much easier to learn.

When you get these vital things under your belt you become self-sufficient and are ready to take it to the next step. But don't worry if you think you're not learning it fast enough, many guitarists have spent countless hours pulling their hair out trying to figure out and understand the guitar.

I strongly recommend practicing a little bit of fretboard navigation in the mornings if possible. If you do that, it will stay in your mind throughout the day. The more you do it, the clearer it will become.

You may forget some things here and there, but if you practice consistently, it will all come together like a jigsaw puzzle.

Just stick with it.

Remember: Quality over Quantity.

Ten minutes of quality practice far outweighs the benefits of one hour of aimless noodling around.

Set a timer on your phone for an amount of time to focus 100% and not get distracted. For me, it is about ten minutes before I start to think about food or that jerk that cut me off in traffic earlier.

When you start to feel like you are not concentrating anymore make sure to stop what you're doing, have a short break, and set the timer again. You can continue where you left off or practice something different.

If you desperately want to achieve a particular chord change, scale, or picking technique, then short bursts of high concentration practice is the way to go. If you're struggling with speed and accuracy, slow it down and get it perfect, then gradually increase the speed of the metronome. Remember: ALWAYS use a metronome.

Most importantly, have fun and find ways to enjoy the struggle. The rewards will be worth it.

Get this next sentence tattooed on your brain:

You WILL get there. I've never seen anyone fail at guitar if they stick with it.

The Song Pyramid

All the songs I want to play, including my originals, go on to the pyramid. Once I determine their spot—easy, medium, or hard—I work at moving them down the pyramid and eventually out of it all together.

It's a very efficient way to get a lot of songs on your playlist. The best way to map out your pyramid is on a whiteboard in your main practice area.

Make sure you spend time in each area and don't neglect any sections as doing so will have a negative effect on your progress.

Too much time spent practicing hard songs will just leave you frustrated and burn you out. This is a quick way to end up in a guitar rut, shatter your progress, and lose interest.

Too much time spent in the easy section will ultimately make you bored and less keen to play guitar. It might leave you thinking that you're a much better player than you are and you'll get a reality check when you go to a jam.

Challenge yourself in the hard section and have fun polishing your skills in the easy section.

I suggest spending most of your practice time working on the easy and medium songs and reserve the hard songs for when you're inspired and up for a good challenge.

Don't burn yourself out in the hard section but don't neglect it either.

The more songs you work on and move down into the easy part of the pyramid, the better you become. Only add songs to the completed list once you can play them comfortably from start to finish, but don't neglect them once they're there. Practice them regularly to ensure they remain part of your arsenal forever and not back in the pyramid.

Add songs as you please and don't feel to compelled to finish songs that you've started if you're not feeling them anymore. Another way to end up in a rut is to force yourself to keep learning a song you're not into anymore. Remove songs from the pyramid to keep it fresh.

PRACTICE MINDSET

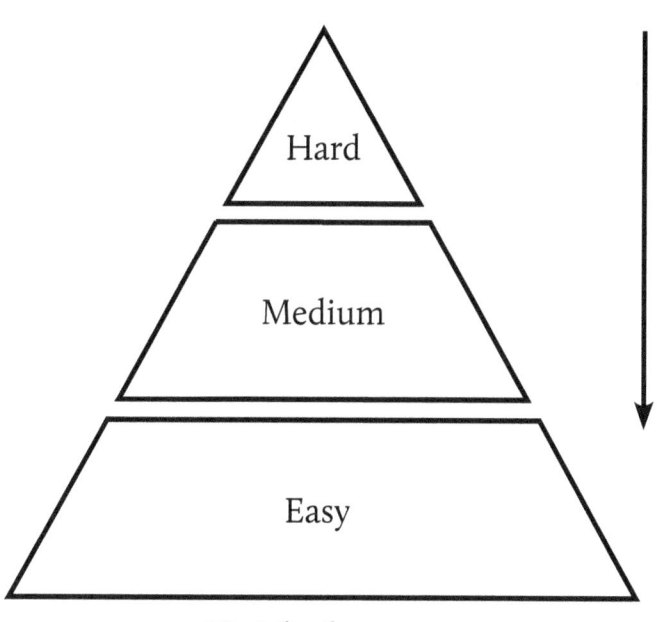

Finished songs:

The Bottom Line

You've probably worked out by now that I'm crazy about the guitar.

Hopefully after reading through this chapter, you've gained some inspiration to start forming some solid practice habits.

The bottom line is: if you want it bad enough, you will make it happen. Cut out the time-wasting habits, stop scrolling on your phone, and, like Slash says, "plug the F#*% in".

PRACTICE MINDSET

STRANGER IN THE DARK

Breaking free from that bad habit of rubber necking over the fretboard is essential for any intermediate player to progress to a more advanced level.

You don't see rock stars gazing over at the fretboard constantly. That's because they have trained their senses and harnessed the power of muscle memory through a lot of repetition.

The more you do it the easier it will become.

Not only will it improve your posture, fret hand, and strumming hand accuracy, but practicing in the dark will force you to feel and hear your way around the fretboard. Doing this regularly will improve dexterity and naturally train your ears and hands to work in unison.

It doesn't matter if you hit the wrong notes, just move your fingers around until you find the right note or string. It will feel strange at first and you will make mistakes, but you can only get better the more you do it.

> ***This is the hardest and least enjoyable part of my practice routine; it is also the most beneficial.***

Always set a timer and try not to play too many different things during that time, just focus on two or three different songs, scales, chords, riffs, or whatever it is you want to play.

The benefits of "stranger in the dark" are endless and I do it some nights before bed. Not only does it improve posture and fret and strumming hand accuracy it also makes me tired and helps me get to sleep much quicker.

Thirty minutes of practicing in the dark late at night is about the equivalent of meditation; it'll whisk you away into another realm and you'll feel your whole body and brain slowly shut off. Your hands will become automatic, playing the music that that flows through your body without even thinking about it. Repetition is the key here and by being consistent you will become a weapon on the guitar.

If you get stuck on what to practice, here are a few ideas:

Practice changing between open chords and then progress to the CAGED system, covering the entire fretboard. If you're unfamiliar with the CAGED system, there's plenty of good tutorials on YouTube.

Put on a metronome and practice dexterity exercises like the spider walk up and down the neck.

Practice playing while standing up.

Make it the final thing you do before bed and the first thing you do when you wake up. Just ten minutes twice a day will supercharge your progress.

If practicing late at night, drink some chamomile tea before starting, get ready for bed, brush your teeth, set your alarm, and make your bed. That way, when you are finished, you can just slide into bed and be out like a light within minutes.

Record some of your stranger in the dark sessions so that you can listen back and review your performance. This is a good idea for all practice sessions as it allows you to identify certain areas that need to be worked on.

Try to release the tension and relax your hands. Good posture should become automatic as you won't be peering over at the fretboard.

If you practice stranger in the dark during the day, make it impossible to see the fretboard by putting on a blindfold.

It might seem pointless at times, but improvements to your playing will be noticeable. The making of a guitar god involves practicing the hard parts most of us like to avoid.

It will feel like a chore at first and you'll want to avoid it, but it needs to be done. Stick with it and be patient and consistent. It will pay big dividends.

THE DEEP END

It's time to bite the bullet and play in front of others. You're already a half-decent player and YOU CAN pull something together. Even if it is not perfect, it doesn't matter.

> ***The difference between a master and beginner is that the master has failed more times than the beginner has even tried.***

All that time practicing alone means nothing if you don't share it with people. Your confidence will skyrocket every time you play in front of others and it will motivate you to practice more.

Let's face it: guitarists love showing off.

An essential part of being a musician is gaining the confidence to play in front of people, so pencil it into your 90-day progress diary as one of your goals.

One of the first times I got up and played to an audience was at a karaoke night in the camp where I was working. I was a nervous wreck, but once I started to play "Killing in the Name Of" with the song playing in the background it felt awesome. I knew it wasn't perfect while I was playing and that I was missing some notes, but the small crowd loved it.

If you're playing in front of people who are drinking alcohol—which is quite often the case—your music will sound better the more festive everyone gets. If you can manage to bust out some simple two or three chord classics, you'll get people singing along. It's a great feeling when the people you're performing to get involved.

Check for open mic nights in your area and just book it in. Choose a song you can play from start to finish and practice it every day in the lead up to the big night, but remember that it doesn't have to be perfect. You will be surprised at how supportive and encouraging the music community is, and people who don't play and are just there to watch will always give you compliments. Missing a note or a chord is not a big deal if you play with passion. Making mistakes will make you want to practice even more to get it right next time.

If your nerves are getting the better of you and you just can't do it, then go anyway just to watch some of the other performers. You will learn a lot by watching other people have a go.

Gigs are also good places to find other like-minded musicians to jam with on a regular basis. It could be the start of something big. The best thing about jamming with others and performing is the amount you learn. Don't get intimidated by better players, be inspired by them.

Bottom line is you just have to do it or it will eat away at you forever. If you shy away from performing too much, your confidence will diminish and you'll end up practicing less and lose interest. Us guitarists all have dreams of playing on stage in front of a crowd.

You got this!

www.ingramcontent.com/pod-product-compliance
Lightning Source LLC
LaVergne TN
LVHW021741060526
838200LV00052B/3399